Shine Songbook and CD
2016–17

Compiled for the *Shine: Living in God's Light* curriculum

MennoMedia
Harrisonburg, Virginia
Kitchener, Ontario

Brethren Press
Elgin, Illinois

Shine Songbook and CD, 2016–17, is published for use with Primary, Middler, Multiage, and Junior Youth during the 2016–2017 curriculum year. *Shine: Living in God's Light* is published by Brethren Press and MennoMedia. Rose Stutzman, project director.

Songbook credits: Chad Thompson (p. 1), Susan Harden (p. 4), Gabhor Utomo (p. 9), Kate Cosgrove (pp. 10-11), Len Epstein (p. 15), Keith Neely (p. 17), Rebecca Thornburgh (p. 23), Gary Undercuffler (p. 24), and David Miles (pp. 28-29), illustrators; Chrissie Walls, Mary Ann Weber, and Rachel Nussbaum Eby, editors; Dan Stutzman, music engraver; Merrill Miller, senior designer. Song credits are listed with each song.

CD credits: Produced and arranged by Jacob Crouse and Seth Hendricks. Recorded by Jacob Crouse at Happy Corner Church of the Brethren and Jacob Crouse Productions. Additional recording by Zach Erbaugh. Mixed and Mastered by Jacob Crouse. All instruments by Jacob Crouse and Seth Hendricks except trombone by Erica Adler, violin by Paul Apts, and mandolin by Ethan Setiawan. Vocalists: Erica Adler, Jeff Adler, Christy Crouse, Jacob Crouse, Zach Erbaugh, Dwayne Henderson, Seth Hendricks, Dallas McVey, Wendy Noffsinger-Erbaugh, Gloria Ruemping, Karen Runck, and Jonathan Timmons.

Contents

Track numbers below refer to the tracks on the CD found in the pocket of this songbook.

Aleluya Y'in Oluwa (Alleluia, Praise the Lord)

Traditional Nigerian song

Angels We Have Heard on High

Glo - - - - - ri-a in ex-cel-sis De - o, Glo - - - - ri-a in ex-cel-sis De - o.

Words: unknown, *Nouveau Recueil de Cantiques,* 1855; tr. unknown
Music: traditional French carol, *Nouveau Recueil de Cantiques,* 1855

As I Went Down to the River

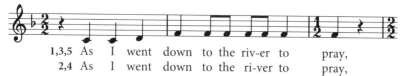

1,3,5 As I went down to the riv-er to pray,
2,4 As I went down to the ri-ver to pray,

stud-y-in' a-bout that good old way, and who shall wear the
stud-y-in' a-bout that good old way, and who shall wear the

Fine

star - ry crown. Good Lord, show me the way.
robe and crown. Good Lord, show me the way.

1 Oh, sis - ters, let's go down,
2 Oh, bro - thers, let's go down,
3 Oh, fa - thers, let's go down,
5 Oh, sin - ners, let's go down,

let's go down, come on down.
let's go down, come on down.
let's go down, come on down.
let's go down, come on down.

Oh, sis - ters, let's go down,
Come on, bro - thers, let's go down,
Oh, fa - thers, let's go down,
Oh, sin - ners, let's go down,

D.C

down to the riv - er to pray.
down to the riv - er to pray.
down to the riv - er to pray
down to the riv - er to pray.

4 Oh, moth-ers, let's go down, come on down, don't you

wan - na go down. Come on, moth - ers,

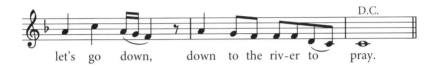

D.C.

let's go down, down to the riv-er to pray.

American folk song

Emmanuel, God with Us

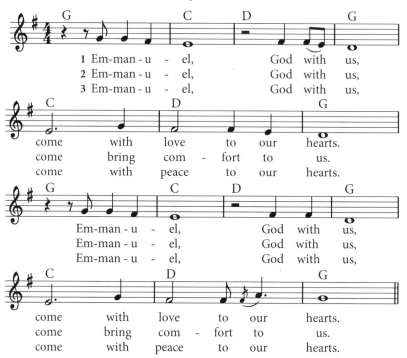

1 Em-man-u - el, God with us,
2 Em-man-u - el, God with us,
3 Em-man-u - el, God with us,

come with love to our hearts.
come bring com - fort to us.
come with peace to our hearts.

Em-man-u - el, God with us,
Em-man-u - el, God with us,
Em-man-u - el, God with us,

come with love to our hearts.
come bring com - fort to us.
come with peace to our hearts.

Words and music: Monica Brown
© 2002 Monica Brown and Emmaus Productions

Fluye, Espíritu, fluye (Flow, Spirit, Flow)

1 Flow, Spir - it, flow,
2 Flu - ye, E - spí - ri - tu, flu - ye,

do what you will do, I
haz lo que quie - ras ha - cer, yo me o-

of - fer myself for you to use as you will,
fres - co pa - ra que me us - es co-mo quie-ras,

flow, Spir - it, flow.
flu - ye, E - spí - ri - tu.

Public domain

God of the Bible

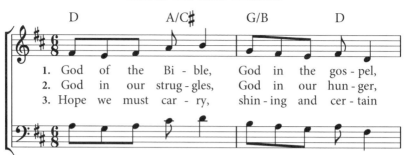

1. God of the Bi - ble, God in the gos - pel,
2. God in our strug - gles, God in our hun - ger,
3. Hope we must car - ry, shin - ing and cer - tain

hope seen in Je - sus, hope yet to come,
suf - fer - ing with us, tak - ing our part,
through all our tur - moil, ter - ror, and loss,

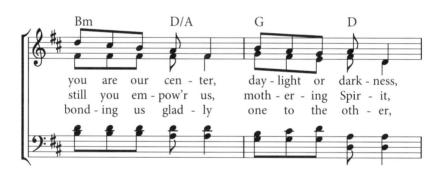

you are our cen - ter, day - light or dark - ness,
still you em - pow'r us, moth - er - ing Spir - it,
bond - ing us glad - ly one to the oth - er,

free - dom or pris - on, you are our home.
feed - ing, sus - tain - ing, from your own heart.
till our world chang - es fac - ing the cross.

Guide My Feet

Leader

1. Guide my feet
2. Hold my hand
3. Stand by me
4. I'm your child

All

while I run this race,

yes, my Lord!

guide my feet
hold my hand
stand by me
I'm your child

while I run this race,

yes, my Lord!

guide my feet
hold my hand
stand by me
I'm your child

while I run this race, for I

don't want to run this race in vain! (race in vain!)

African-American spiritual

I'm Gonna Sing

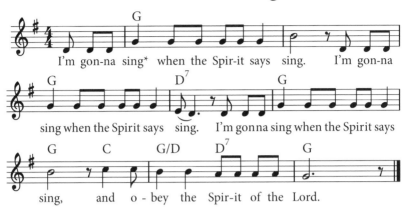

I'm gon-na sing* when the Spir-it says sing. I'm gon-na

sing when the Spirit says sing. I'm gonna sing when the Spirit says

sing, and o - bey the Spir-it of the Lord.

*2: pray, 3: cry, 4: shout

African-American spiritual

I've Got a Friend

o-ver the world and that is why we   say: We've got a

friend who cares for,   friend who cares for   us.

Words: Cynthia Breeze
Music: Cynthia Breeze and Debra Sutter

Jesus, Be the Center

Words and music: Michael Frye

Let Us Love

1. Let your love shine down, let your love shine down, let your love shine down on me, on me. Let your hope roam free, let your hope roam free, let your hope roam free with me, with me. Let us love, let us hope, not in word or speech, but let our ac - tions lead the way.

2. Let your truth be shown, let your truth be shown, let your truth be shown to me, to me. Let your peace rain down, let your peace rain down, let your peace rain down over me, over me. Let there be truth, let there be peace, not in word or speech, but let our ac - tions lead the way.

Words and music: Seth Hendricks and Michael Good

Longing for Light

Christ, Be Our Light

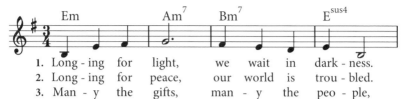

1. Long - ing for light, we wait in dark - ness.
2. Long - ing for peace, our world is trou - bled.
3. Man - y the gifts, man - y the peo - ple,

Long - ing for truth, we turn to you.
Long - ing for hope, man - y de - spair.
man - y the hearts that yearn to be - long.

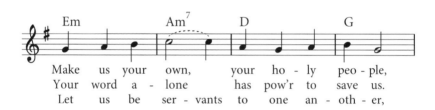

Make us your own, your ho - ly peo - ple,
Your word a - lone has pow'r to save us.
Let us be ser - vants to one an - oth - er,

light for the world to see.
Make us your liv - ing voice.
mak - ing your king - dom come.

Christ, be our light! Shine in our

Christ, be our light!

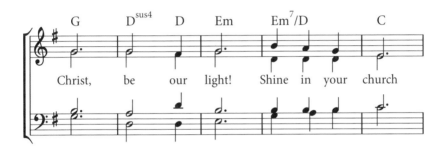

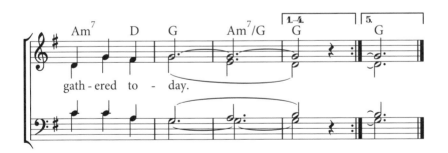

Word and music: Bernadette Farrell
Christ, Be Our Light (80229) © 1993 Bernadette Farrell.
Published by OCP Publications, 5536 NE Hassalo, Portland, OR 97213

The Lord Lift You Up

Words and music: Patricia J. Shelly

© 1983 Patricia J. Shelly, arranged by Dennis Friesen-Carper

Love God and Your Neighbor

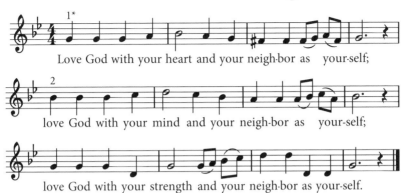

Love God with your heart and your neigh-bor as your-self;

love God with your mind and your neigh-bor as your-self;

love God with your strength and your neigh-bor as your-self.

*may be sung as a round

Words: from the Gospels
Music: traditional

May the God of Peace

May the God of peace give you peace. May the

God of hope give you hope. And may the

God of love fill your heart with end - less love.

Words and music: Monica Brown
© 2011 Monica Brown

Now Our God

1. Now, our God, we give thanks to you, for all the things you have
2. Now, our God, we give love to you, for all the things you have
3. Now, our God, we give praise to you, for all the things you have

done. You've shown your grace in so man - y ways, your
done. You've shown your grace in so man - y ways, your
done. You've shown your grace in so man - y ways, your

mer-cy and kind-ness and pow'r. We thank you, thank you,
mer-cy and kind-ness and pow'r. We love you, love you,
mer-cy and kind-ness and pow'r. We praise you, praise you,

thank you, Lord, we thank you, thank you, thank you, Lord.
love you, Lord, we love you, love you, love you, Lord.
praise you, Lord, we praise you, praise you, praise you, Lord.

Words and music: Ralph P. Merrifield

Say to the Lord, I Love You

Words and music: Ernie Rettino
© 1981, 2006 Rettino/Kerner Publishing

Siyabonga, Jesu (Thank You, Jesus)

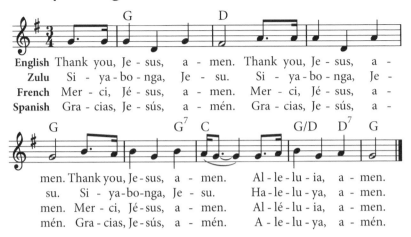

English Thank you, Je-sus, a - men. Thank you, Je-sus, a -
Zulu Si - ya-bo-nga, Je - su. Si - ya-bo-nga, Je -
French Mer - ci, Jé-sus, a - men. Mer - ci, Jé-sus, a -
Spanish Gra - cias, Je-sús, a - mén. Gra - cias, Je-sús, a -

men. Thank you, Je-sus, a - men. Al - le - lu - ia, a - men.
su. Si - ya-bo-nga, Je - su. Ha - le - lu - ya, a - men.
men. Mer - ci, Jé-sus, a - men. Al - lé - lu - ia, a - men.
mén. Gra - cias, Je-sús, a - mén. A - le - lu - ya, a - mén.

Music: traditional Southern East African

Uyai Mose (Come All You People)

Ostinato Refrain

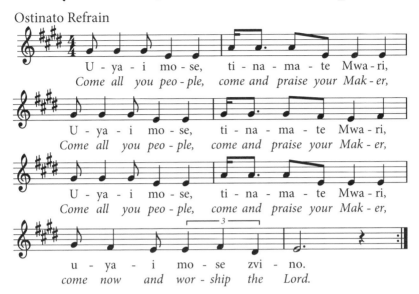

U - ya - i mo - se, ti - na - ma - te Mwa - ri,
Come all you peo - ple, come and praise your Mak - er,

U - ya - i mo - se, ti - na - ma - te Mwa - ri,
Come all you peo - ple, come and praise your Mak - er,

U - ya - i mo - se, ti - na - ma - te Mwa - ri,
Come all you peo - ple, come and praise your Mak - er,

u - ya - i mo - se zvi - no.
come now and wor - ship the Lord.

Words: Alexander Gondo
Music: Alexander Gondo, arr. John L. Bell, © 1994, Iona Community, GIA Publications, Inc., agent

We Welcome Glad Easter

1. We wel-come glad Eas-ter when Je-sus a-rose,
2. We tell how the wom-en came ear-ly that day,
3. We sing of the an-gel who said: "Do not fear!
4. We think of the prom-ise which Je-sus did give:

and won a great vic-to-ry o-ver his foes.
and there at the tomb found the stone rolled a-way.
Your Sav-ior is ris-en, and he is not here."
"That he who be-lieves in me al-so shall live!"

Then raise your glad voic-es, all Chris-tians, and sing,

bring glad Eas-ter prais-es to Je-sus, your King.

Words: anonymous
Music: Welsh hymn tune

Woza Nomthwalo Wakho
(Come, Bring Your Burdens to God)

Pronunciation: Woh-zah nohm twah-loh wah-koh (3x), oo Jeh-zwah-kah soh zah tee hay.

Words: traditional South African, transcr. Barbara Clark, Mairi Munro, and Martine Stemerick

Music: traditional South African melody from the singing of the Mooiplaas congregation, arr. Welile Sigabi

Copyright © 2008, WGRG, Iona Community, Scotland. GIA Publications, Inc., agent.